WHAT'S THE STORY

First published in 2025 by OH
An Imprint of HEADLINE PUBLISHING GROUP LIMITED

1

Disclaimer:

Cataloguing in Publication Data is available from the British Library

ISBN 978-1-03542-949-3

Compiled and written by: Malcolm Croft
Editorial: Claire Castle
Designed and typeset in Avenir by: Stephen Cary
Project manager: Russell Porter
Production: Rachel Burgess
Printed and bound in China

Headline's policy is to use papers that are natural,
renewable and recyclable products and made from wood
grown in well-managed forests and other controlled
sources. The logging and manufacturing processes are
expected to conform to the environmental regulations of
the country of origin.

HEADLINE PUBLISHING GROUP LIMITED
An Hachette UK Company
Carmelite House, 50 Victoria Embankment, London EC4Y 0DZ

The authorised representative in the EEA is Hachette Ireland, 8 Castlecourt Centre,
Dublin 15, D15 XTP3, Ireland (email: info@hbgi.ie)

www.headline.co.uk   www.hachette.co.uk

WHAT'S THE STORY

THE LITTLE GUIDE TO
OASIS
UNOFFICIAL AND UNAUTHORISED

CONTENTS

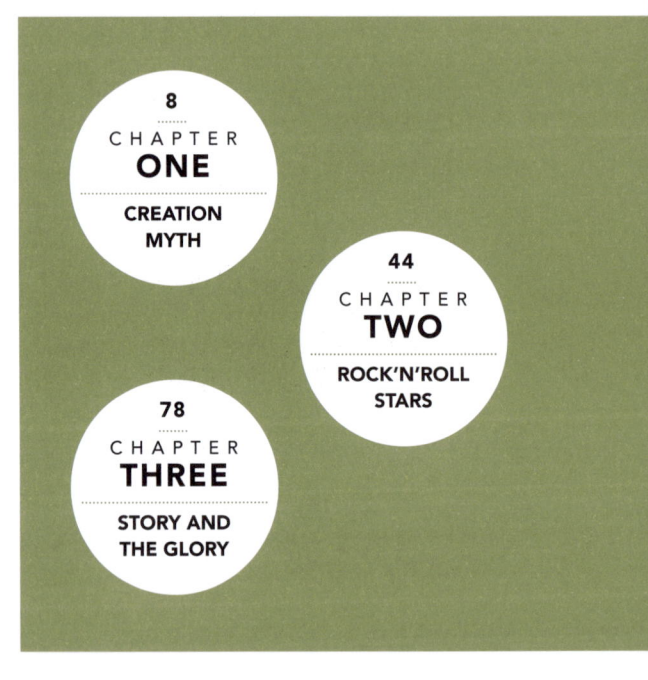

INTRODUCTION

It's happened! Finally! After 15 years of looking back in anger, Noel and Liam Gallagher, the heart and soul of Oasis, finally agreed it's getting better, man, and acquiesced to give their fans what they never thought possible – a fookin' reunion!

Since 2009, the Gallaghers' public squabbles in interviews and social media have grown in increasingly hilarious (and hurtful) ways, keeping fans uncertain whether the band would ever share a stage again. The pair, along with the rest of Oasis, of course – a revolving cast of shadows, except for Bonehead – are responsible for two of the most successful British albums ever made – *Definitely Maybe* and *(What's the Story) Morning Glory?* – and scores of hits still familiar to millions.

For those that dare to remember, between 1994–1999 Oasis were invincible. They gave an entire generation a soundtrack of anthems to sing and swear by, as well as a pair of real rock 'n' roll stars they could finally relate to. (Funny bastards, too, as you'll soon see.) Along the way, Oasis courted controversies as often as possible, so it came as little surprise when Noel decided to slide away in 2009, causing fans all around the world to start crying their hearts out and getting their parkas all wet.

Fifteen years later, and on the eve of *Definitely Maybe's* 30-year anniversary, the "Oasis Live '25" reunion was revealed. It gave their loyal and patient fans the morning glory they all deserved. How long the reunion lasts is anyone's guess, so it's probably best to just roll with it!

What's the Story is the greatest hits of the band's best wisdom and wit, the ideal companion for when you feel mad for it and need to soak up some supersonic swagger in the sunshiiiiiiiiine.

So, go grab your cigarettes & alcohol and pop that champagne supernova while you're at it, because Oasis are back… and this time they're gonna live forever.

CHAPTER
ONE

CREATION MYTH

In 1993, two years after their debut show in Manchester, this now-legendary rock band – fuelled by the Beatles, cigarettes & alcohol, and Colombia's whitest export – signed a record deal with Alan McGee's Creation Records.

It would be an era-defining moment, not just for Oasis, but for the rest of "Cool Britannia" too. Pop on your parka and bucket hat, it's time to dive back into the 90s…

Stone Roses 1989. I was in the crowd and I thought 'Fuck this, I'm off to do it myself.'

Liam, on his inspiration to form The Rain, his first band, *The Telegraph*, August 1997

We were pretty nervy, but Liam immediately had that stance behind the microphone. He had that presence on stage immediately. There were probably about 10 people in the room, but there might have been 10,000 in the room in Liam's head.

Bonehead, on The Rain's first gig at Manchester's Boardwalk club in August 1991, *Mojo*, December 1995

Liam and Bonehead's band, The Rain, were formed in Manchester in 1991 with original members Liam, Paul "Guigsy" McGuigan, Paul "Bonehead" Arthurs and drummer Tony McCarroll.

They played their first gig on 14 August 1991, at the Boardwalk club, Manchester.

Noel was in the crowd and liked the songs he heard – "Alice", "Take Me" and "Reminisce" – all written by Liam and Bonehead, but never recorded.

I didn't know anybody else who
I would desire to be in a band with
except these four guys. It's as simple
as that. It's fate I suppose.

Noel, on forming Oasis out of Liam's band, The Rain,
interview with Caspar Llewellyn Smith in August 1994,
published in *Observer Music Monthly*, 4 September 2009

There was 40 people maximum there and we had a song called 'Rock'n'Roll Star'. People were sniggering and going 'Yeah, course you are, mate, bottom of the bill at the Boardwalk on a fuckin' Tuesday night.' Pretentious arseholes is what they thought we were. We went down like a fucking knackered lift. We thought they were going to be in raptures. And it ended in this bowl of silence.

Noel, on Oasis's first ever gig*, interview with Phil Sutcliffe, Q magazine, February 1996

* After Liam's band, The Rain, debuted live in August 1991 at the Boardwalk club, Noel joined the group and changed the band's name. Oasis's first gig with Noel was on 19 October 1991, also at Manchester's Boardwalk.

At first, we thought, 'Everyone hates us and we don't care'. Now we know everyone doesn't hate us really, and we do care a little bit!

Guigsy, on the band's response to their almost immediate success, *Bassist* magazine, January 1998

I'm the songwriter, the brains behind the band, the quiet, calm one. Liam's the nutcase, and then there's the other three. The tunes are really good and catchy, but the lyrics are shit. I don't think that attitude's ever gonna change, so I'm arsed, me.

Noel, when asked to introduce the members of Oasis, *Select*, 11 August 1996

Everyone expected Oasis to finish within 18 months; even ourselves, originally, because we couldn't see how we could carry on. Now we can't see an end to it.

Guigsy, on the group's reputation and longevity, *Bassist* magazine, January 1998

"

I'm not a pop star. I'm a rock'n'
roll star. And I'm mad for it. **"**

Liam, on being mad for it, *NME*, 12 July 1997

I'm a miserable twat sometimes.
See, all the stuff on *Definitely Maybe*
was written when we didn't have
a record deal and I wasn't writing with
anything in mind… But now, when
I write I think of what all the people…
are going to read into it… Now we're
a business.

Noel, on struggling with the lyrics for songs on
(*What's the Story*) *Morning Glory?*, interview with
Ted Kessler, *NME*, 24 June 1995

You've got to do it, you know what I mean? You can be a fucking knob like Joe Strummer and say you're never going to do *Top of the Pops*. You've got to get on and do it and try and be as fucking big as you can. It's all about ambition, innit?

Noel, on *Top of the Pops*, and ambition, interview with Caspar Llewellyn Smith in August 1994, published in *Observer Music Monthly*, 4 September 2009

I've got GCSEs in music and in life and you don't get them from school. You get them from eating your porridge.

Liam, on porridge (and leaving school without qualifications), *The Telegraph*, 16 August 1997

After the first four gigs in Manchester no-one would put us on, because we had this reputation for being difficult. We had a fight with the headlining band one night 'cos they pulled the plug on us during the last song… It got us a bit of a reputation.

Noel, on the band's early reputation as scrappers, interview with Simon Williams, *NME*, 4 June 1994

They were just an indie band before I joined. It was all right, it just wasn't rock'n'roll. But the bassist looked good, the drummer didn't look too bad, and our kid looked pretty fucking cool… So I bowled into the practice room one day and said, 'Right, change that guitar, take them shoes off, cut your hair, I'm gonna be doing this from now on.' And they just looked at me and said, 'Oh, all right, then.'

Noel, on joining The Rain, Liam's band with Guigsy, Tony McCarroll and Bonehead, interview with Simon Williams, *NME*, 4 June 1994

I always used to bash about on this guitar, playing stuff like 'Hey Jude'. Then I saw The Smiths and I said, 'That's it! That's the way I want to play guitar.' Then after that I saw John Squire from The Stone Roses cross them two with Paul Weller and John Lennon and that's how I wanted to sound.

Noel, on the origin of Oasis's signature guitar sound, *PEOM*, 19 June 1994

I fucking hate sleeping, me.
Boring! I wish I didn't have to
sleep, it's such a waste of time.
I'd rather be up, living.

Liam, on sleeping and partying, *NME*, 12 July 1997

All the songs on that album were written when I was on the dole and I had fuck all going for me. I was writing about escaping. I wasn't writing about being on the dole and how shit it was. I was writing about how great it could be if we were in a band. That's what people who come to the gigs can relate to cause we're singing about them.

Noel, on the lyrical themes of *Definitely Maybe* and fans relating to them, interview with Caspar Llewellyn Smith in August 1994, published in *Observer Music Monthly*, 4 September 2009

Wibbling Rivalry

During an April 1994 interview with *NME* journalist John Harris, Noel and Liam were recorded on tape arguing hilariously for more than 14 minutes. The tape, titled "Wibbling Rivalry", was released by independent label Fierce Panda in 1995, just after the release of "Wonderwall". (Both brothers approved the release of the tape.)

At one point during the argument, Liam lays into Noel: "I fuckin' hate him. And I hope one day… I can smash fuck out of him, with a fuckin' Rickenbacker, right on his nose, and then he does the same to me, 'cause I think that we're stepping right up to it now. There's a fuckin' line there and we're right on the edge of it," somewhat eerily predicting the events that would lead to the band's demise in 2009.

I ain't the voice of a generation for anyone and neither is anyone in the band. We're not figureheads of any movement and we don't aspire to be. People are saying we're the most important band since blah blah blah and that's their opinion. We're not going to say, 'No we're not'.

Noel, on Oasis being considered the voice of a generation, interview with Caspar Llewellyn Smith in August 1994, published in *Observer Music Monthly*, 4 September, 2009

[We're] the best bits of every band that anyone's ever liked. We sound like all the important bands. People slag us off and say we sound like the Beatles, T-Rex, the Stones, Jam, Sex Pistols, but it's better than sounding like Spandau Ballet.

Noel, on the group's influences, interview with Caspar Llewellyn Smith in August 1994, published in *Observer Music Monthly*, 4 September, 2009

With Oasis, like the Roses and the Mondays, it's the bottom line: here's a guitar, here's the songs, you have them. We're not preaching about ye olde Englande or how it was in the 60s. We're not preaching about our sexuality, we're not telling people how to act.

Noel, on Oasis's basic attitude to music and fans, interview with Simon Williams, *NME*, 4 June 1994

It was fucking hysterical, like Beatlemania or something! We've only had one single out - what's it gonna be like when we get an album out?

Noel, on an infamous Coventry University gig when fans mobbed the stage, interview with Simon Williams, *NME*, 4 June 1994

[Liam] wants to be remembered like Sid Vicious, while I just want to be a great songwriter. He thinks I'm boring and soft and he can't understand that you change.

Noel, on the age difference between him and Liam, interview with Cliff Jones, *The Face*, August 1994

Before that? Fucking fish-tank maker.
I worked in a bakery. As a signwriter.
As a labourer. Worked in a dry cleaners.
You fucking name it, I done it…
Why the fuck would I aspire to be a
fucking fish-tank maker?… You do
what you have to do, because your
mam boots you out of bed at 11 o'clock
in the morning and says, 'Get down
the fucking job centre!'

Noel, on his early careers before founding Oasis,
interview with Caspar Llewellyn Smith in August 1994,
published in *Observer Music Monthly*, September 4, 2009

[I wrote 'Acquiesce'] on the way to the sessions for 'Some Might Say'. The train stops in the Severn Tunnel... for 2.5 hours. I had my acoustic guitar. By the time I got there, it was written. There was only one woman in the first-class compartment. She said, 'What are you doing?' I went, 'I'm writing a song.'

'Gosh!' she says, 'Are you in a pop group?' and I go, 'Yeah, I'm in Oasis actually.' She goes, 'I suppose my daughter's probably heard of you.' I thought, 'Yeah, I've probably shagged her.'

"

Noel, on writing "Acquiesce", arguably the band's greatest B-side, interview with Tom Sheehan, *Melody Maker*, 27 April 1996

If it was that easy every fucker would be doing it… I believe everyone's got special talents, it's just a matter of finding it, realising what it is and then getting on with it and doing it. I was always told when I was young, there's no point in playing that guitar because you're just going to end up working in in Maccy D's. It was like, no. Fuck that.

Noel, on being a great songwriter and growing up in Manchester, interview with Caspar Llewellyn Smith in August 1994, published in *Observer Music Monthly*, 4 September 2009

While Noel was fascinated by music in his teens, Liam was not. He was only into football. That all changed in 1986, when he was 14 and he was hit over the head with a hammer by a teenage boy from another school. He recalled the event in May 2022 to *The Guardian's* Rich Pelley:

"My girlfriend at the time was really into Madonna. She'd play 'Like A Virgin' and I'd say: 'I'm not having this shit.' Then I got hit on the head with a hammer and thought: 'This is actually a tune.' I ended up in hospital and, after that, I just started hearing music differently. So whoever hit me, I'd like to meet and thank, else I'd still be on the dole."

From 1991 to 2024*, Oasis sold more than 75 million albums globally and more than 10 million in singles sales, including eight UK No.1s.

These are the group's Top 10 biggest-selling singles in the UK:

1. "Wonderwall" – 3.6 million sold!
2. "Don't Look Back In Anger"
3. "D'You Know What I Mean"
4. "Whatever"
5. "Roll With It"
6. "Live Forever"
7. "Some Might Say"
8. "Stop Crying Your Heart Out"
9. "Stand By Me"
10. "Cigarettes & Alcohol"

* Following the reunion announcement in August 2024, *Definitely Maybe* re-entered the UK charts at No.1.

If it wasn't for us, fucking Echobelly and Shed Seven would be the most important bands in Britain... and that would be a farce.

Noel, on Britpop competition, interview with Caspar Llewellyn Smith in August 1994, *published* in *Observer Music Monthly*, 4 September, 2009

Nothing gets me down about life in general, nothing pisses me off. I'm ambidextrous, I write with my left hand and I play guitar with my right. I'm right-footed, I'm double-jointed in one elbow: I'm the most bizarre character ever. So nothing amazes me. If I see a spaceship land I won't get freaked out. I'll just say, 'What kept ya?'

Noel, on his cheery disposition and aliens, interview with Caspar Llewellyn Smith in August 1994, *published in Observer Music Monthly*, 4 September, 2009

'Supersonic' is about some fucking nine-stone geezer who got Charlie'd off his nut one night… it's not about anything! It's just about a feeling, you just get up and play it.

Noel, on the lyrics of "Supersonic", interview with Simon Williams, *NME*, 4 June 1994

In 20 years' time our album *Definitely Maybe* will still be in the shops and that's what it's about. In 20 years' time people will buy the album and listen to it for what it is. They won't listen to it because we were rock'n'roll.

Noel, on *Definitely Maybe's* legacy, interview with Caspar Llewellyn Smith in August 1994, published in *Observer Music Monthly*, 4 September, 2009

All I want is to do my gigs, sing my songs, have a couple of pints and go on holiday with my family and my missus.

Liam, on his desire to live a simple life, interview with Rich Pelley, *The Guardian*, 26 May 2022

CHAPTER
TWO

ROCK'N'ROLL STARS

Following the release of their debut record *Definitely Maybe* in 1994, Oasis were catapulted from Burnage, a borough of Manchester, to become the leading shaker makers of alternative rock.

With ambition as big as their arrogance, Oasis had arrived. The world has yet to sober up…

Before we came along, success was a dirty word. We kind of reinvigorated ambition. As dumb-arse a message as it was, looking back now, it was 'Things are shit, so we might as well celebrate something – let's celebrate being young.'

Noel, on ambition and arrogance, interview with Neil McCormick, *The Telegraph*, 8 February 2007

The singer's an arrogant git, I'd like to twat him one. And the rest of the band might as well be cardboard cutouts… but… the songs! Aren't the songs FUCKING GREAT!?

Noel, on his thoughts about Oasis, interview with Simon Williams, *NME*, 4 June 1994

[Maine Road] was the beginning of the end. After that we were so big we had no control of the vehicle anymore.

Noel, on the Maine Road shows of April 1996, *MOJO*, March 2000

Oasis's most treasured hometown show was at the stadium ground of their beloved Manchester City, Maine Road, on April 27, 1996.

The setlist is rather incredible:

1. "The Swamp Song"
2. "Acquiesce"
3. "Supersonic"
4. "Hello"
5. "Some Might Say"
6. "Roll With It"
7. "(What's the Story) Morning Glory?"
8. "Round Are Way"
9. "Cigarettes & Alcohol"
10. "Champagne Supernova"
11. "Whatever"
12. "Cast no Shadow"
13. "Wonderwall"
14. "The Masterplan"
15. "Don't Look Back in Anger"
16. "D'Yer Wanna Be a Spaceman?" (aborted)
17. "I Am the Walrus"

Encore: "Cum On Feel the Noize'

Knebworth was just a money-spinner…
Three million applied for tickets.
It wasn't necessarily an enjoyable
experience because all these people
had come from all over and we
weren't that hot live, there. 99

Noel, on the sold-out two nights at Knebworth in
August 1996 (250,000 fans attended), *MOJO*, March 2000

At Knebworth I thought we were doing one night and we were doing two. I got that mashed on the first I woke up to a knock on the door and thought I was at home. I forgot all about it. But I had to go and do it again. That was heavy.

Liam, on performing two sold-out shows to 125,000 people a night at Knebworth, 10–11 August 1996, *Alan Carr's Chatty Man*, 1 July 2011

After Knebworth we should've gone
on holiday for a couple of months…
[But] a week later we were on a
plane to fucking America, playing
in front of 10,000 people. Which
is not good for your ego.

Liam, on touring the United States after the success
of Knebworth, *Select*, August 1997

I think the sound of *Definitely Maybe* was a bit one-dimensional, everything was the same tone, whack it up to ten and off we go. There's a lot more variety in the songs and a lot more going on generally on *(What's The Story) Morning Glory?*

Noel, on the difference between the first and second album, interview with Ted Kessler, *NME*, 24 June 1995

" Noel is good. But I'm better. **"**

Liam, on Noel, *Addict*, 1 February 1995

I mean on a song like 'Wonderwall'; Tony would never in a million years have been able to drum like Alan did.

Noel, on the difference between original drummer Tony McCarroll and his replacement Alan White, *Musician*, July 1996

The band's name – Oasis – came from a tour poster for the Inspiral Carpets that was hung on Noel and Liam's bedroom wall. One of the venues listed on the poster was Oasis Leisure Centre, in Swindon, a venue Liam played with his band Beady Eye in 2011.

However, that wasn't the only influence for the band name as Liam told the *NME* in 2013:

"It was a shit name, but most band names are shit. There was a shop in the Manchester Arndale Market called Oasis… and there was a taxi rank round the corner called Oasis."

I'd like to think when I'm 56, I'll just disappear with a bit more grace. It's not the most dignified business we're in here, but I think I'd rather go out of business. What is the point of working when you're 50 years of age? [Mick Jagger's] been at it for 30 years. Put your feet up, go and make some cocoa and shut the fuck up man!

Noel, on retirement and aging rock stars, *Melody Maker*, 7 March 1998

I don't really see me at the Borderline playing a mouth organ to 150 people on a Wednesday. Every time I write a song, I envisage them in football stadiums with loads of people going fucking mental. And that's Oasis.

Noel, on his ambition for Oasis's songs and his songwriting, interview with Neil McCormick, *The Telegraph*, 8 February 2007

He's the singer of the band. And it was his group before I joined so I'm hardly gonna kick him out am I? Plus what else is he gonna do anyway, he'd only be hanging around the house, getting under someone's feet… You have to remember he's only 25. He's still a young kid. If you were 25 and in one of the biggest bands in the world you'd probably be a bit of an arsehole as well.

Noel, on Liam and his "mad for it" reputation, *Melody Maker*, 7 March 1998

"
I can only do this one way: with me in complete control of it. **"**

Noel, on being the de facto chief of Oasis, *The Guardian*, 22 April 1995

I see it as three albums and that's it…
I don't think I can do any more with
Oasis after that… There's [only] so
many anthems you can write.

Noel, on his masterplan of ending Oasis after three
albums, interview with Ted Kessler, *NME*, 24 June 1995

The best book I ever read was *The Lion, The Witch And The Wardrobe*, when I was ten… I love the idea of opening a cupboard door, you step inside and there's a lion and you're being chased through the snow.

Liam, on reading books, *GQ*, February 1998

Nothing bothers me more than when groups like Pearl Jam and Nirvana whine and moan and complain about life and being famous. Let me tell you, being famous is great! If you hate your job so much, why don't you fucking go work at a car wash or McDonald's?

Noel, on the American grunge bands prevalent in the nineties and cracking America, BBC, April 2008

Oasis are probably the last of the
big – and I use this term because
I can't think of another – 'alternative'
bands to really make an impact
on the country.

Noel, on Oasis's legacy, *Dotmusic,* July 2002

People want to know why… I'm always shouting at people or punching photographers and it's because I'm not like one of these celebrity dicks. I don't need my gob in the gossip pages. I make music and you either like it or don't. That's it. Don't follow me down the shop.

Liam, on paparazzi and fans invading his space, *The Observer*, 16 June 2002

All that tabloid stuff is a pain in the arse, isn't it?… I'd rather they wrote about me than some other dick though. I'm interesting.

Liam, on being a constant fixture in the tabloid press for being a "bad boy", *NME*, 12 July 1997

Writing songs, that's what gets me going. Not the drugs or the sex or the rock'n'roll behaviour, it's the music. I write all the time. I've got the attention span of a fucking gnat so if I'm not doing something like writing or doing interviews I just sit there vegetating, fucking taking drugs.

Noel, on music and his attention span, interview with Caspar Llewellyn Smith in August 1994, published in *Observer Music Monthly*, 4 September 2009

In hindsight it was the best thing that ever happened to us. If someone had said to me that two founder members would leave… I would have thought, 'I'm not too sure about this'. But the guys leaving was a problem for the night it happened. But I woke up the next day and I thought, I know Gem (Archer) isn't doing anything, and then we found out that Andy (Bell) was available.

"

Noel, on Bonehead and Guigsy leaving the band in 1999, *MOJO*, March 2000

I really think that the legalisation of drugs… over 25 years probably would be a great thing because it would take the romance and the rebel element out of it for kids. But that 25-year [period] would be fucking utter chaos and disaster and scandal after fucking drug-addled scandal.

Noel, on the legalisation of drugs and its possible side effects, *Rolling Stone*, May 2015

I'd say to God, 'You've heard "Don't Look Back In Anger?"', and he'd say, 'Of course.' I'd say, 'Look it's me, let us in. I can play you a tune. I robbed some stuff, I took a lot of drugs, but I'm all right.'

Noel, on what he'd say to God if/when he gets the chance, *The Sun*, January 2013

As hellraiser, I'd say that I was way below average, but as rock star, I'm probably quite interesting. It depends on whether you like me or not. If you don't, then you'll probably think, 'Stupid twat, I hope he dies.'

Noel, when asked "How do you rate yourself as a rock star?", *Melody Maker*, December 1998

I think everyone knows by now
I don't consider myself to be
[a great lyricist, but]… Well, 'I'm
the best lyricist in Oasis' is the
way I like to say it.

Noel, on his reputation as a lyricist, interview with
Paul Du Noyer, *The Telegraph*, 7 November 1998

The 90s was not the beginning of something – it was the end of something. It was the end of the music business as we knew it. We were the last rock stars.

Noel, on Britpop and the music industry of the 1990s, *Radio X*, September 2012

People call me a celebrity. Bollocks! I'm a singer! You never see me down film premieres even though I get invited to about a hundred a week. I hate standing there with all those knobs coming in, in dresses they've borrowed. Fuck off!

Liam, on not being a celebrity, *The Observer*, 16 June 2002

Americans want grungy people stabbing themselves in the head onstage. They get a bright bunch like us, with deodorant on, they don't get it.

Liam, on touring the United States, *NME*, November 2006

I don't want to be experimenting as well – 'Let's try this in an urban cybersonic punk style.' No, give us that Marshall stack and that guitar. I know where I am with that, thank you very much.

Noel, on the group's signature sound and reputation for lack of experimentation, interview with Neil McCormick, *The Telegraph*, 8 February 2007

I don't think we were a Britpop band, we were just Oasis.

Liam, on nineties Britpop, *Filter*, 10 April 2005

C H A P T E R
THREE

STORY AND THE GLORY

After Noel Gallagher completed recording his second masterpiece, *(What's the Story) Morning Glory?* – only a year after *Definitely Maybe* – little could he predict, despite his overwhelming confidence, that he would become one of Britain's greatest living songwriters.

The album was not just his splendid morning glory, it was his crowning glory too…

This is a true story. I actually went to see them at The Water Rats in Kings Cross and thought they were fucking great, but I didn't like the drummer. Three weeks later I was in the band. Someone up there was watching over me.

Alan White, on joining Oasis in 1995 ahead of the recording *(What's the Story) Morning Glory?*, *Rhythm* magazine, 15 July 2000

66

I think you have, too. Good luck signing on.

99

Noel, to Guigsy's very brief bass replacement, Scott McLeod, who appears in the "Wonderwall" music video. After McLeod quit, he told Noel he thought he'd made the wrong decision, *The Guardian*, 19 June 2004

You gotta have ambition.
Think penthouse, not bedsit. **"**

Noel, on his ambition, *Hotpress*, 6 September 1994

I've been there, bought the T-shirt.
If you ever need to have a chat about
anything, I'm your man.

Liam, on being a man of the world, *Esquire*, April 2022

The Who always play 'I Can't Explain'; and we'll always play 'Wonderwall'. People ask us if we get bored of it. You can't get bored of 15,000 people shouting for 'Wonderwall'. That's better than drugs. You get a hard-on when you hear that.

Noel, on playing "Wonderwall" at every live show, Q magazine, December 1999

> **"**
> # It keeps the wolf from the door.
> **"**

Noel, after being told that his first three albums had sold a combined 27 million copies, *Melody Maker*, 7 March 1998

I like Noel outside the band. Human Noel – that's my brother – I fucking adore him and I'd do anything for him. But the geezer that's in this fucking business, he's one of the biggest cocks in the universe.

Liam, on Noel, *NME*, 5 June 2013

I am a tender, beautiful and
loving guy that happens to slap a
photographer now and then because
they get in my way.

Liam, on Liam, sky.com, July 2005

Interviews are an occupational hazard… You're sat in a room with some guy from Stockholm who you've never met and he's asking you about your mum. It's fucking preposterous. Because the honest answer to that is: 'What's it got to do with you?' But the smart answer is always: 'I liked her until she gave birth to Liam.'

Noel, on media interviews, his mother and Liam, *The Guardian*, 5 August 2019

I suppose I do get sad, but not for too long. I just look in the mirror and go, 'What a good-looking fuck you are.'

Liam, on Liam, *NME*, November 2006

A perfect day for me would be not being me… I'd go down the shops in the West End and check out all the places I can never go in. I've only been down Oxford Street once. It was a few years ago after an awards ceremony. It was three in the morning. And I got arrested. The only time I ever see the street is from a car. I spend my whole life being driven around… I'm not here to moan but it would be nice to be able to go for a walk.

Liam, on his perfect day, *The Observer*, 16 June 2002

It's made him pull his finger out and work for a living at last. He's selling more records and way more tickets than me so good luck to him, ride it until the wheels come off.

Noel, on Liam's successful post-Oasis career, interview with Sam Delaney, *The Big Issue*, November 2019

I think it's good being a bit dangerous. There's a few more kids going out going, 'Fuck it, I can have what I want out of life.'

Liam, on his reputation for being wild, and being a role model, *Rolling Stone*, 18 May 1995

Fame is great for about a year. Then it just becomes too much. And you can't back out, you're stuck with it.

Noel, on the perils of fame, interview with Miguel Cid, *Heat* magazine, 24 February 2000

I only know five people who haven't taken drugs and that's my mam, me gran, me father-in-law, me mother-in-law and my newborn baby. Everyone else, lawyers, doctors, or what have you, they've all got their heads down once in a while. Nothing wrong with it, all part of growing up.

Noel, on drugs, *NME*, 26 February 2000

He wanted to spend more time
with his family. He has two kids up
in Manchester and he wanted to be
with them – so we let him go.
It's hardly Paul McCartney leaving
The Beatles.

Noel, about Bonehead leaving the band in March 1999,
NME, 10 July 1999

They're my songs. I wrote them all by myself and I'm proud of them and I'm proud of what they mean to other people and I'm proud of where they sit with what I've done now. **99**

Noel, about his prolific catalogue of Oasis and solo songs, *DIY*, July 2011

The title of Oasis's biggest hit single is, of course, "Wonderwall".

The song was written about Noel's then-girlfriend (soon-to-be wife), Meg Matthews.

Noel borrowed* the title from George Harrison's *Wonderwall Music*, an instrumental soundtrack album he released in 1968, the first album released on the Beatles' record label, Apple Records.

* The title of the band's debut album, *Definitely Maybe*, was also borrowed, this time from a song called "Definitely Maybe" by the Jeff Beck Group and released in 1972.

It's a dream, really, isn't it? You dream of being on *Top Of The Pops*, you dream of being in the back of posh cars, of not having to pay for anything, of loose women and all the rest of it. That's all come true, so you might as well enjoy it while you can, before it finishes. You're only going to get five years out of all this.

Noel, on being a rock and roll star, *Hotpress*, 6 September 1994

[Would I give Noel a kidney?] Without a doubt. Of course I would. He's my brother, man, and I love him.

Liam, on helping a brother out, *The Guardian*, 26 May 2022

We'll never split up, we're brothers. And if Oasis ends, then it'll end on a high. Who knows? We might still be together in 50 years, still playing music, which'll be nice.

Liam, on Oasis never splitting up, *NME*, 12 July 1997

There comes a point when you just can't do it anymore. You can't go to any more parties, you can't drink any more drinks, you can't do any more drugs. There comes a point when you've just got to go, 'All this has got to change.'

Noel, on quitting drugs, interview with Paul Weller, *The Guardian*, 31 October 1999

As soon as people realise that the majority of people in this country take drugs, then the better off we'll all be. Taking drugs is like getting up and having a cup of tea in the morning.

"

Noel talking about drugs, BBC Radio 1, January 1997

Ewan McGregor was my neighbour, right, and he came round my house the night he got the part of Obi-Wan Kenobi. I just happened to have two of those lightsaber toys, so I said, 'Come on – in the back garden.' And we had a fucking lightsaber fight. His first Jedi training session was with yours truly in my back garden at eight in the morning.

Noel, on practising *The Phantom Menace* with Ewan McGregor, interview with Holly Pine, *Shortlist*, 16 October 2011

Oasis make it look all very simple, but they've worked extremely hard.

Noel, on Oasis's work ethic, *PEOM*, 19 June, 1994

People are prepared to have stand-up rows with me in the street: 'I fucking love that album!' And I'm like, 'Mate, look, I wrote the fucking thing. I know how much effort I put into it. It wasn't that much. It's the sound of five men in the studio, on coke, not giving a fuck.'

Noel, disowning *Be Here Now*, *The Guardian*, *6 October 2016*

I took all the tour money and a big bag of drugs and went to stay with a young lady friend of mine. I wrote it about brief experiences of running around America for a week. At least something positive came out of it: a great fucking song.

Noel, on writing "Talk Tonight" after taking a brief break from the band after a massive row with Liam in Los Angeles during the first American tour in 1994, *The Sydney Morning Herald*, 30 November 2006

It's just me and my brother having arguments in a band. If we weren't in a band, we'd be havin' it in the house. If we had a greengrocers, Gallagher's Greengrocers, we'd argue over which way we set out the apples or the fuckin' pears.

Liam, on arguing with his brother, *Rolling Stone*, 18 May 1995

"

Things started to go pear-shaped after we'd finished recording *Standing On The Shoulder Of Giants*, and Noel, Liam and I had to find two new guys to replace them. We weren't actually that worried, because we knew there would be thousands of guitarists and bassists who would want a job in Oasis. What was important, though, was to get people in that we knew, and who fitted into the band on a personality level.

"

Alan White, on Guigsy and Bonehead leaving the group in 1999, *Rhythm* magazine, 15 July 2000

Not being loved and not being able to love. That's my biggest fear.

Liam, on his biggest fear, *Q* magazine, May 2020

I don't know who the guy is who's in these interviews, he seems really cool, because the guy I've been in a band with for the last 18 years is a fucking knobhead.

Noel, on how Liam handles press interviews, *Herald Sun*, October 2008

If you're given a blank cheque to record an album and as much studio time as you want you're hardly gonna be focused. Especially if there's a pub round the corner and Kentucky Fried Chicken – you just get lazy.

Noel, on *Be Here Now*, Q magazine, December 1999

CHAPTER
FOUR

D'YOU KNOW WHAT I MEAN?

Over the years, Noel and Liam Gallagher have showcased their sarcastic, swaggering and often scattergun sense of humour in hundreds of iconic interviews, giving their fans a lot more to love them for than just the songs.

Today, the brothers are renowned for their hilarious wit and wisdom, not only in ripping the merciless piss out of each other, but also anything else that pisses them off too...

Me and Bonehead would just walk into a hotel room and empty it out the window.

Noel, on the early days of partying hard,
The Guardian, 22 April 1995

I was in my bedroom. Winter time. It went G, E minor, C, D, the basic chords, right, and the chorus was, 'And life goes on, but the world will never change'. I must have been smoking too much pot at the time. It was, I dunno, just to see if I could do it. After that I wrote about 75 songs no one's ever heard.

Noel, on writing his first ever song as soon as he'd learned a third chord, interview with Phil Sutcliffe, Q magazine, February 1996

[Andy and Gem] had to step into Oasis in its prime, just like I did, and hats off to them because they've done a great job. And it feels good not to be the 'new' boy anymore.

Alan White, on Guigsy and Bonehead leaving the group in 1999, *Rhythm* magazine, 15 July 2000

Every songwriter in a band wants to do a solo record, just to see if you can do it on your own, and I know I can do it on my own. And it would be nice to do it in a stress-free environment, without fucking Liam running around the studio with ten cans of Guinness and a bottle of Jack Daniels, fucking knocking things over.

Noel, on recording a solo record, *Total Guitar*, December 1998

Now I know what the word big means. We thought we were big when we played Earls Court, then Maine Road. But after last night... There's big, then there's bigger than big, and then there's fuckin like last night... Now that is big. Now that is big. It's big.

Noel, summing up the August 1996 Knebworth shows, *Select*, 11 August 1996

Signing autographs doesn't change you... When I go on [stage] at a gig at night, all that shit, fame and stuff, just goes out your head.

Liam, on fame and the importance of playing gigs, interview with Tom Sheehan, *Melody Maker*, 27 April 1996

Liam is… rude, arrogant, intimidating and lazy. He's the angriest man you'll ever meet. He's like a man with a fork in a world of soup.

Noel, on Liam, and soup, Q magazine, April 2009

I've literally got nothing left to write about. I've wrote about being a youth, and I've wrote about being a rock star, and I've wrote about living life in the big city.

Noel, on songwriting and inspiration, BBC Music 6, 29 October 2010

If they want to hear old Oasis songs, they're being played by a fat man in an anorak somewhere with shorts on, you know, so they can go and see that. I've no desire at all to get back involved with Oasis.

Noel, on Liam* performing Oasis songs and the Oasis reunion, *Wired*, June 2019

* Liam responded on X, rather hilariously: "There's banter and then there's banter but slagging of a man's anorak is out of order." @liamgallagher, 21 June 2019

I don't mind it. Fans turn up wanting pictures. It's cool, man. No one's tried to kill me yet. But bring it on!

Liam, on his fans/assassins, *NME*, 8 June 2013

I'm constantly brushing my teeth.
Whenever I walk past a toothbrush
I'll have a little go.

Liam, on brushing his teeth, *The Face*, September 2019

23 August 1996

The date Liam infamously refused to turn up to the taping of Oasis's *MTV Unplugged*.

Despite claiming he had a sore throat, Liam in fact simply sat in the balcony of London's Royal Festival Hall and heckled Noel between songs, while drinking beer and smoking.

"As they said, 'Ladies and Gentlemen, Oasis', we walked out and Liam wasn't there", Noel told *Far Out* magazine. "He said, 'I'm not doing it.' And I thought, 'Thanks a lot.'"

Noel sang lead vocals for the 12-song set instead of Liam, and knocked it out the park.

I'm not really a frontman – I'm a
backing vocalist. At Oasis gigs, I would
sing one in every six songs – to give
Liam's voice a rest, the poor flower –
and that was always a nice change.
I just hope people are prepared for
me singing for an hour and a half. But
I'm trying to get it out of everyone's
heads that I left the band to 'go solo'.
That's not my preferred explanation
for why I'm doing this.

Noel, on his first live gigs as Noel Gallagher's
High Flying Birds, interview with Holly Pyne, *Shortlist*,
16 October 2011

I don't listen to his albums because I can't stand his voice… I think it's unsophisticated music. For unsophisticated people. Made by an unsophisticated man. Who's giving unsophisticated orders to a load of songwriters who think they're doing the Oasis thing.

Noel, about Liam's band, Beady Eye and solo albums, interview with Tim Jonze, *The Guardian*, 5 August 2019

One of the worst things that ever happened to me was when I said that thing about Blur [in an interview in 1995, Gallagher said he hoped Damon Albarn and Alex James would 'get Aids', which he later apologised for]. My mam rang me up when she saw that and she was really angry and she said to me 'I didn't bring you up to talk like that.'

Noel, on his cruel comment to Damon Albarn and Alex James, *The Irish Times*, 3 October 2008

I fucking hate Glastonbury, mate.
I'm only here for the money. It's
fucking shit. I've got to wear
fucking wellies.

Liam, on headlining Glastonbury with Oasis in 2004,
NME, July 2004

Glastonbury has a tradition of guitar music and even when they throw the odd curve ball in on a Sunday night you go, 'Kylie Minogue?' I don't know about it. But I'm not having hip hop at Glastonbury, no way man. It's wrong.

Noel, on his infamous quote about hip-hop artist Jay-Z headlining Glastonbury 2008, *The Guardian*, 15 April 2008

130

My lyrics don't mean that fuckin' much. 'You've gotta roll with it' – what the fuck does that mean?

Noel, on the lyrical quality of his songs, *Select*, 11 August 1996

I've always been a songwriter, but I didn't have a vehicle for the songs. Just me and a guitar. I didn't know anybody else. As soon as I saw the others playing I knew this was it. **99**

Noel, on joining Oasis in 1991, *Hotpress*, 6 September 1994

I think we're both the problem and the problem is that [Noel] thinks he's not the problem.

Liam, on which one of the Gallaghers is the problem, interviewed by Jonathan Ross, *The Jonathan Ross Show*, 28 November 2020

I have me bad days, but that's life, innit? I had good days when I was on the dole and I had bad days when I was on the dole. I have great days being here and I have bad days being here. As long as I know there's a gig coming up, I'm sweet as. That's what it's all about.

Liam, on his mental health and happiness playing with Oasis, interview with Tom Sheehan, *Melody Maker*, 27 April 1996

We have sold more records than The Beatles. We've played bigger gigs than The Beatles. I will say, yeah, we are bigger than The Beatles, man.

Noel, on Oasis being bigger than the Beatles, *Select*, 11 August 1996

Sweden – in the hotel with Primal Scream and The Verve. We got deported and banned. Thirty grand damage. All fookin' great memories!

Noel, when asked about the most debauched night while on a leg of a European tour, interview with Tom Sheehan, *Melody Maker*, 27 April 1996

I just knew that if we did a few gigs and got a bit of interest, that'd be it. It would just go fookin' mad. And as soon as 'Supersonic' come out, it did.

Liam, on his confidence of Oasis's success after the release of the debut single "Supersonic", interview with Tom Sheehan, *Melody Maker,* 27 April 1996

[Noel] goes, 'I've heard you're a good little drummer. We're sacking ours; do you want to be in my band?'… He asked me to meet him for a drink, so I met him in a cafe in Camden, and there he was, sitting outside with his bottle of Becks. 'You must be the boy', he said. And that was it, I got the job. Then it was *Top Of The Pops* the next day.

Alan White, on getting the gig as Tony McCarroll's replacement, *Rhythm*, February 1996

Whoever said I'm on a line of cocaine every 40 minutes, I'll sue the fucker. That's out of order. In Oasis, Guigsy, Bonehead and Alan White don't take drugs. Me and our Liam do. We'll take anything that's put in front of us because that's just the kind of guys we are… I wish I'd never started smoking cigarettes or drinking beer or taking cocaine or ecstasy because I'd have a lot more money.

Noel, on his and Liam's expensive drug use, interview with Phil Sutcliffe, Q magazine, February 1996

There's no faking. I'm me.
I sniffed cans of gas at the age of
12. Took mushrooms at the age
of 12 – proper mushrooms. Not
20. More like 150. I've done all
that. You walk out of a gaff with
a fucking bottle of Jack Daniel's
and people reckon you're on
that rock'n'roll myth thing.

I do it because I'm onto it.
I won't change – not unless the
geezer with the big beard lands
down in front of me and pulls
a giraffe out of his nostril and
goes, 'I'm God - you've got
to be like this, you've got to be
like that.'

"

Liam, on being a genuine rock'n'roll star,
The Sunday Times, 18 February 1996

Being Liam Gallagher keeps me down-to-earth.

Liam, on what keeps him grounded, *Rolling Stone*, 18 May 1995

It was either get in a band or get drunk every night.

Bonehead, on why he chose to start a band, *Rolling Stone*, 18 May 1995

When [Liam] was at school, he was quite normal. Now he's definitely mad. He's mental. He's not mad like some people in bands are mad. That fucker's mad. Mad. He's madder than mad… He's just mad.

Noel, on Liam, *The Guardian*, 22 April 1995

If I wasn't a musician I don't know.
I'd be God, maybe? That would be
a good job.

Liam, on what becoming something other than
a musician, quoted in *Shortlist*, 27 August 2024

" I thought we'd be the Stones, doing it until the day we died. For it to implode like that was disastrous. **"**

Liam, on the Oasis split in 2009, *Readers Digest*, July 2022

If there were gold medals for taking drugs for England I would have won a shitload.

Noel, on drugs, specifically his taking of them in large quantities, interview with Michael Parkinson, *Parkinson*, ITV chat show, 25 November 2006

CHAPTER
FIVE

LIVE FOREVER

As Oasis swagger back into our lives in '25 (and hopefully beyond), let's take a moment to look back in happiness and reflect on all the good times the band gave us before Oasis Mark 2 comes to town.

These are the moments that are gonna live forever…

In August 2009, Noel quit Oasis after a physical fight between the brothers broke out backstage before a performance at the Rock En Seine festival, Paris.

According to Noel, Liam lunged at him violently while allegedly wielding an acoustic guitar like an axe.

With only four shows left on the *Dig Out Your Soul* tour, Noel walked out, but not before posting a message on the band's website.

It's with some sadness and great relief to tell you that I quit Oasis tonight. People will write and say what they like, but I simply could not go on working with Liam a day longer.

Noel, writing on the band's website immediately after he walked out, August 2009

I see myself as one of the fucking true great rock'n'roll singers on the planet.

Liam, on Liam, interview with Eve Barlow, *Noisey*, June 2017

Gem is totally 100 percent into being in a band… In the past it was always me and to a lesser extent Liam, and no one else took an interest in where the band was going. But Gem will come up with 50 ideas of how a song should be in about a minute. Gem's enthusiasm sort of pushes everyone along.

Noel, on Gem Archer, the group's new guitarist from 1999, cnn.com, 19 July 2002

The thing between me and Liam, is ... he can bullshit to other people and they believe him and I can bullshit to other people, but we can't bullshit to each other because we've known each other for too long

Noel, on Liam, interview with Caspar Llewellyn Smith in August 1994, published in *Observer Music Monthly*, 4 September 2009

As soon as I got some money, I was out of there. In Manchester I was sick and tired of going into pubs I'd been going into since I was 15 and everyone saying, 'Tight bastard!' if I didn't buy the drinks and 'Flash Bastard!' if I did. I was sick and tired of young crack heads coming up to me in clubs and sticking a screwdriver in me back and saying, 'On your next tour… we're going to be your security team.'

Noel, on the reasons why he felt compelled to leave Manchester for London, interview with Phil Sutcliffe, Q magazine, February 1996

Andy is the most talented musician out of all of us... He usually says about two or three sentences in an afternoon, but they are probably the most important ones in the whole afternoon.

Noel, on Andy Bell, the group's new bassist from 1999, cnn.com, 19 July 2002

I said everything I ever wanted
to say in 'Rock'n'Roll Star'.

Noel, on the lyrical message of "Rock'n'Roll Star",
interview with Phil Sutcliffe, Q magazine, February 1996

It's a myth that Liam and I are at each other's throats all the time. I can't be bothered anymore. I've backed out of all the fighting. I'm the champion and that's the end of it.

Noel, on his spats with Liam, *Nuts*, 21 January 2005

I think the band as a whole should have called it a day, after we played Knebworth. That had to be the pinnacle of the band's career, and for me personally I had taken it further than I could ever have imagined.

Bonehead, on quitting Oasis in 1999, poptones.co.uk, 10 May 2005

What I will say, though, is if the shit hits the fan and all this stops tomorrow, I'm Bonehead's daughter's godfather, right, and I'm Liam Gallagher's brother, and I'm Paul McGuigan's best friend, and I'm Alan White's best friend. We are a family. Whatever I've got, they can have.

Noel, on the band being a family, interview with Phil Sutcliffe, Q magazine, February 1996

If we were to sit down now and take John Lennon, Jimi Hendrix, Ray Davies, Steve Marriott, anybody's first two albums against my first two albums, I'm there. I'm with The Beatles. If you ask me where I'll be after my eighth album in comparison to The Beatles, then they'll piss all over me. Probably.

Noel, on the classic status on *Definitely Maybe* and (*What's the Story) Morning Glory?*, interview with Phil Sutcliffe, Q magazine, February 1996

When I'm writing a song I'll
sit up in a chair for 48 hours,
smoking, drinking, playing the
same line over again… When
I'm going through all that, them
chaps are in their cosy beds,
with their cosy lives – it's all
cosy for them. And when it's
time to make a new album,
they wake up in the morning
and go, 'Where's the songs?'

It's me who has to come up with them. It does come naturally to me, but you've got to fucking work your bollocks off, man, and I do. I live this band 24 hours a day. 🙰

Noel, on the hardships of being the group's solo songwriter in the early days, interview with Phil Sutcliffe, Q magazine, February 1996

I didn't get where I am today without losing a lot of friends in Manchester through being so driven by my own songwriting.

Noel, on his ambition during the group's formative days in Manchester, interview with Phil Sutcliffe, Q magazine, February 1996

People ask what it's like being in a band with your brother and I think, 'What about being on a building site in January when it's hailstoning with your dad, your two brothers, two of our cousins and two of your uncles… and you fuckin' hate the lot of them?

Noel, on being in a band with his brother (over choosing the alternative), interview with Phil Sutcliffe, Q magazine, February 1996

Liam's a fucking brilliant frontman and he stamps his authority over everything he sings. It's his. I can't even come close.

Noel, on Liam, and which he songs he sings over Noel, interview with Phil Sutcliffe, Q magazine, February 1996

I remember playing it to them on an acoustic guitar one night… and it's one of the greatest moments I've ever had as a songwriter. They were just completely and utterly fucking speechless. If I hadn't had the songs, they'd probably have told me to fuck off.

Noel, on playing "Live Forever" to the group for the first time when he joined Oasis, interview with Phil Sutcliffe, Q magazine, February 1996

I quit and got a job with a building firm who subcontracted to British Gas. And the pivotal moment of my entire life was this: a big steel cap off an enormous gas pipe we were laying fell on my right foot and smashed it to bits. When I came back from the sick, they gave me a cushy job in stores handing out bolts and wellies.

Nobody would turn up for days on end. After about six weeks I started bringing me guitars in and I wrote four of the songs from the first album in that storeroom. I look at this foot sometimes in the winter when I get chills in it because of the cracked bones, and I [give it a thumbs up]. 99

Noel, on the injury from a dead-end job that gave him the opportunity to write songs, interview with Phil Sutcliffe, Q magazine, February 1996

Being sat beside Liam on a 15-hour flight. It happened just the once, going to Japan or somewhere. It's just horrible.

Noel, on what he considers to be the worst psychological torture, *Melody Maker*, December 1999

Once, I'd had two days, doing gigs. No food, loads of drugs, loads of drink. I flaked out with chest pains and stayed overnight in a hospital in Detroit. The doctor said, 'You're 27, it's a good job you're not 47, cos you'd be dead.'

Noel, on partying too hard while on tour, interview with Tom Sheehan, *Melody Maker*, 27 April 1996

The music press thought we were great, but the national newspapers said we were a disgrace to our country. Which is fine by me, because our country is a disgrace to us. **99**

Noel, on the band's reputation, and on Britain, *Musician*, July 1996

I can play drums… and the bass and keyboard. I'm one of the multi-talented annoying people who can pick up two ashtrays and start banging them and get a melody out of it.

Noel, on being multi-talented, interview with Liisa Ladouceur, *Chart*, June 1997

It's like Stella Street, round here:
Jamie Oliver lives up the road. I got
told off for throwing stones at his
windows, pissed-up, asking him to
chuck down some bacon rolls.

Liam, on his famous north London neighbours after
moving to Hampstead in the noughties, interview with
Ted Kessler, *NME*, 23 August 2016

I like to think I keep it real. Liam keeps it surreal, and somewhere between the two we get on all right.

Noel, on brotherly relations with Liam, interview with Neil McCormick, *The Telegraph*, 8 February 2007

He'd put his whole life on hold to get Oasis back together. But every tweet he sends out is another nail in the coffin of that idea. If you think for one minute I am going to share a stage with you after what you've said, you are fucking more of a moron than you look.

Noel, about Liam, and his comments about Noel's then-wife Sara McDonald, interview with Sam Delaney, *Big Issue*, November 2019

To this day, Oasis are the proud holders of three Guinness World Records:

1. Fastest-selling pop album in the UK

(*Be Here Now* sold 663,389 copies in the first three days of its August 1997 release date)

2. Longest run of Top 10 singles in the UK

(22 successive Top 10 singles in the UK)

3. Longest single to reach No.1 in the UK charts

("All Around the World" – 9 minutes and 38 seconds!)

If I lost my hair you would never see me on that stage again, because there's no place for baldness in rock'n'roll.

Liam, on bald rock stars, interview with Jane Graham, *Big Issue*, 29 September 2017

66

She's gutted she couldn't get a ticket.

99

Liam, when asked how his mother Peggy felt about the 2025 reunion, @liamgallagher on X, 6 September 2024

I was going to make up some profound statement in the chorus but I couldn't come up with anything that fitted. Then I just thought 'All my people right here, right now. D'You Know What I Mean? Yeah, Yeah.' Very vague… But I fucking love that line, 'Coming in a mess, going out in style.' We were a bunch of scruffs from Manchester and we're going out in a Rolls Royce.

Noel, on *Be Here Now*'s first single "D'You Know What I Mean?", interview with Phil Sutcliffe, *Q* magazine, September 1997

Whatever next? Robbie Williams turning up on his next record? I'd have to send the police round. Put it this way, Noel lives in a £17 million house. That changes you, I reckon. You have appropriate furniture, appropriate kitchens, appropriate red wine that Bono's recommended. And Damon Albarn becomes your mate. Fair dos, but not for me.

Liam, on Noel becoming pals with Blur's Damon Albarn, interview with Ted Kessler, Q magazine, August 2016

Fuck the sea. I ain't going in that. Fuck that, mate. That ain't meant for us. That's meant for the sharks, and the jellyfish, tadpoles and stuff. 99

Liam, on the sea, interview with Eve Barlow, *Vice*, 9 August 2017

Didn't go into rehab like all me mates did – fucking lightweights.

Noel, on never going to rehab, Q magazine, December 1999

There's a load of geezers dressed in parkas who want you to carry on doing what it is they've kind of missed out on… When I'm in the studio, I don't give a fuck what they want.

Noel, on Oasis fans in Discogs mini documentary, *Who Built The Moon?*, April 2018

It's usually 50 per cent true, 50 per cent the imagination of some fictitious editor. But I wouldn't mind if half the time they were telling the truth and the other half of the time it was positive. But it's usually all negative lies.

Noel, on the band's reported reputation in the press, *Melody Maker*, 7 March 1998

I've heard they really annoy him.
Someone told me the other week
that the only thing that does his nut
in are my tweets. Good. They will
carry on and they will get bigger
and better.

Liam, on annoying Noel via social media, interview
with Ted Kessler, Q magazine, August 2016

Towards the end of Oasis you were always stepping into the unknown because the tambourine player was a bit of a loose cannon and it was like, 'Well is this gig gonna finish?'

Noel, on the final few months of Oasis in 2009 and Liam's behaviour, interview with Dan O'Connell, Radio X, 17 January 2023

I was more disappointed that Oasis split up. I wonder if he was. I've never heard him say he was disappointed about Oasis. No, he's got what he wanted.

Liam, on Noel leaving the band for the final time in 2009, interview with Ted Kessler, Q magazine, August 2016

Since the rise of the coffee shop,
culture has disappeared, don't you
think? People are horrified that
they have to pay for music. Music!
But $20 for two coffees, oh,
absolutely.

Noel, on streaming and coffee, *NPR*, 15 March 2018

I can't envisage the morning
I wake up and think I'd like to spend
two years on the road, arguing all
around the world with Liam.

Noel, on a possible reunion with Liam and getting
the band back together, interview with Sam Delaney,
Big Issue, 18 November 2019

27 August 2024

After 15 long years, Oasis revealed
their much anticipated reunion
on the eve of the 30th anniversary of
Definitely Maybe.

The band announced five dates at
Manchester's Heaton Park and
London's Wembley Stadium initially,
as well as two dates each at stadium
shows in Cardiff, Edinburgh
and Dublin, playing to more than
1.4 million fans in total.

Fourteen million people applied for
tickets in a tour expected to earn the
band more than £100 million.

66
This is it, this is happening.
The guns have fallen silent.
The stars have aligned.
The great wait is over. Come see.
It will not be televised. **99**

@oasis post on X, 27 August 2024